Imagine If...
I Could Calm a Storm

Written by Kathy Speight & Camden Speight

Illustrations by Janis Acampora

A FRIENDS IN ACTION PUBLICATION
GREENSBORO, NORTH CAROLINA

No part of this publication may be reproduced in whole or in part, or stored in a retrieval system, or transmitted in any form or by any means, electronic, mechanical, photocopying, recording, or otherwise, without written permission of the publisher. For information regarding permission, write to FRIENDS IN ACTION Publishing, PO Box 39223, Greensboro, NC 27438-9223.

ISBN978-1-60643-107-8

Text copyright © 2008 by Kathy Speight

Illustrations copyright © 2008 by Janis Acampora

All rights reserved.

Published by FRIENDS IN ACTION PUBLISHING

www.FriendsinAction4Kids.com

Printed in the U.S.A.

Library of Congress Control Number: 2008903131

To Camden and Cooper—

Listen to your heart,
believe in your dreams, and
let your kind actions for others find no boundaries.

-Mom

If you think you can make a difference; if you could do anything you want…
What would it be? You can make a difference in anything for anybody.
Just imagine…

Camden Speight, Co-author

It was a rainy day in September. Camden sadly stared out the window wondering when the skies would clear so he could go out and play. He slumped into his favorite chair, picked up the remote control and turned on the television. He searched the channels for a weather report.

He sat up straighter as he listened to a report about a strong storm, a hurricane named Katrina, which had made landfall on the Gulf Coast of the United States. He learned that people had to leave their homes during the storm. Many of those homes were destroyed, and some families lost all they owned.

They did not even have clean water to drink.

That night Camden thought more about the people who were in the storm.
He wanted to help.

"But how can I make a difference from so far away?"
he wondered to himself.

The next morning, Camden woke up and walked to the kitchen for breakfast. His younger brother Cooper was already at the table eating.

Camden went to the refrigerator to get something to drink.

As he looked on the shelves, he saw several bottles of water. He remembered the news report about people in Louisiana and Mississippi who had **no** water to drink. That's when an idea hit him!

"Mom!" Camden shouted, "We have plenty of water in here. Why don't we send it to the people who were in the hurricane? They don't have **any**!"

Camden's mom looked puzzled. "What are you talking about?"

He explained what he heard the day before and how he wanted to help somehow. "We can just send them our water!" he announced with certainty.

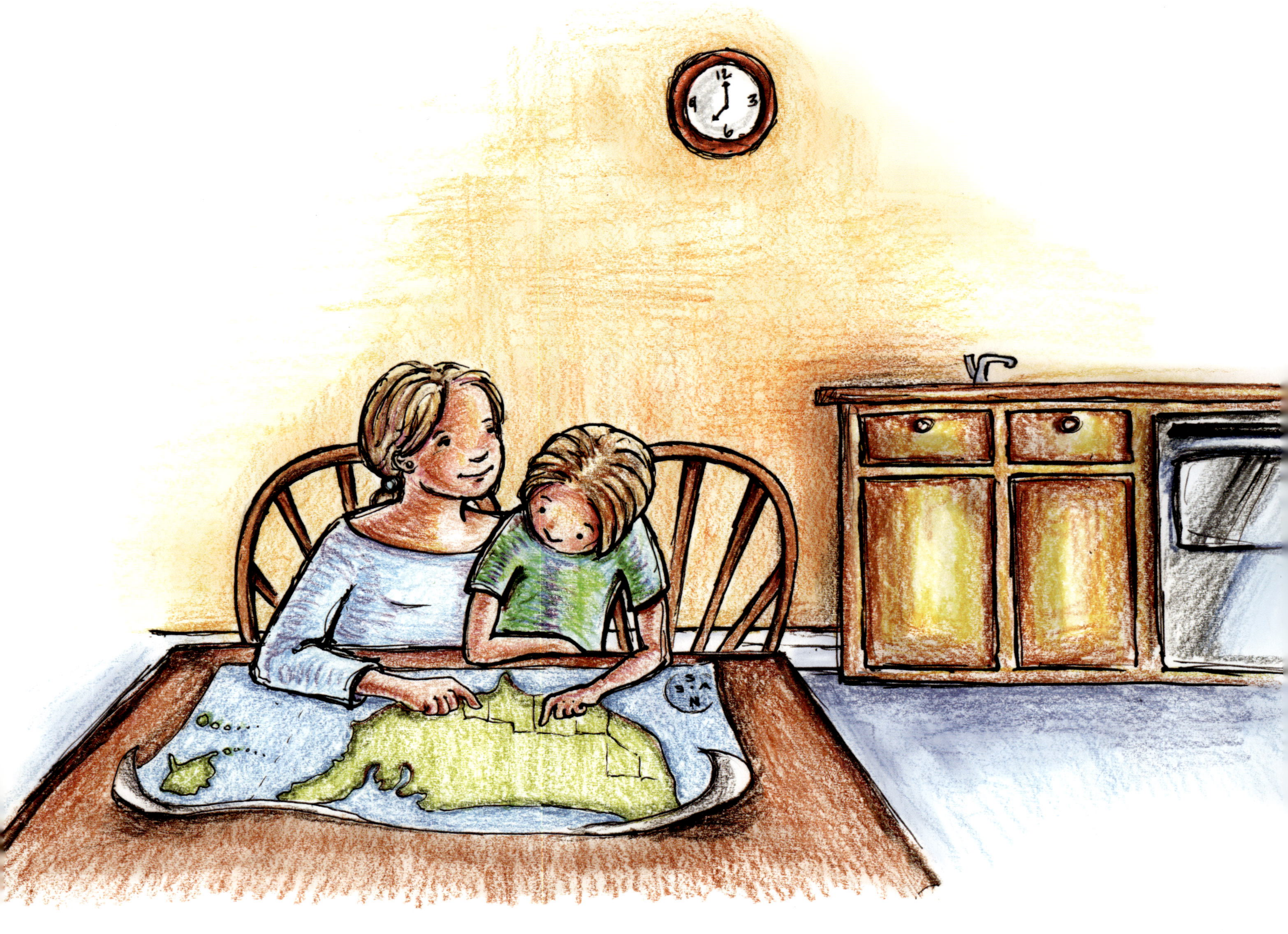

"Let's think through this a bit more," said his mom as they sat down at the table. They looked at a map of the United States, pointing first to North Carolina on the East Coast and then to Louisiana and Mississippi on the Gulf Coast.

How would they ever get the water from their refrigerator to those who needed it? How would just a few small bottles of water help this big problem? They decided to talk more about it after school.

That afternoon they made a plan. "We would have to get all your friends at school to help," said his mom. "Do you think they would?"

Camden knew they would and couldn't wait to get to school the next day to tell them about his project.

"Wow! That's a great plan," said Jack.

"Let's start right away," said Emily. They were going to collect as much bottled water as they could and get their classmates to help. They named their project **WaterWorks**.

When the teachers heard that some of the students wanted to collect water, they felt like helping too.

They encouraged all the first grade teachers and students to bring bottles of water to their classes. When the principal learned what was going on, she encouraged the whole school to participate!

Parents started bringing, not just bottles of water, but **cases** of water to school. Students wrote special notes and drew pictures on labels to put on each bottle. Everyone was getting excited about sending the water.

But how would they get it there?

As word of the children's efforts traveled into the community, Mr. Adams from a local bus company agreed to transport the water. He would have the school load the water onto a newly-built school bus that was on its way to Louisiana.

"I'll be at the school on Friday at 11:00am to get the water," he said.
"Make sure you have it ready."

On Friday, the water was ready to be loaded onto the bus. Camden, his friends and several parents stood outside waiting for Mr. Adams. All of a sudden they heard a commotion behind them and turned around to see what was going on. Students were coming out of the school from every door. Many were carrying more cases of water. The whole school showed up to wait for the bus!

"There it is!" someone yelled from the crowd. Specks of bright yellow could be seen through the trees that lined the school entrance. It seemed like slow motion as the vehicle traveled down the street in front of everyone. Then, the shiny new bus made a left turn into the school's driveway. The entire student body was silent and then all at once, one big cheer erupted as the children welcomed their driver.

They had done it! They came together to collect over 340 cases of water — that's 8,160 bottles of water! Each bottle had a special message of hope written on the label for its receiver.

"Come to NC," said one.

"We're sorry about the storm," said another.

"God bless you," said others.

Some labels had pictures of smiling suns, happy stick people, flowers, or a beautiful new house. Carefully crafted with kindness and care, the bottles of water lined the sidewalk ready for their mission.

"Load that bus! Load that bus!" was chanted as teachers, students and parents loaded case after case of water.

Then, something unexpected happened. The bus was almost full and there was much more water to load.

"What do we do now?"
Camden asked Mr. Adams.

The businessman smiled and said, "I'll take care of it."

He took his cell phone out of his pocket and made a call. About twenty minutes later, another empty bus arrived ready to be filled.

When both buses were packed with water and ready to go, the students waved goodbye to Mr. Adams.

At that moment, their special gifts began the journey to Louisiana.

For many days, Camden and his friends talked about their **WaterWorks** project. They wondered if the bus made it to its final destination.

"Did the water get there?"

"Were people reading what they had written?"

"Did it make them happy to get it?"

They had so many questions.

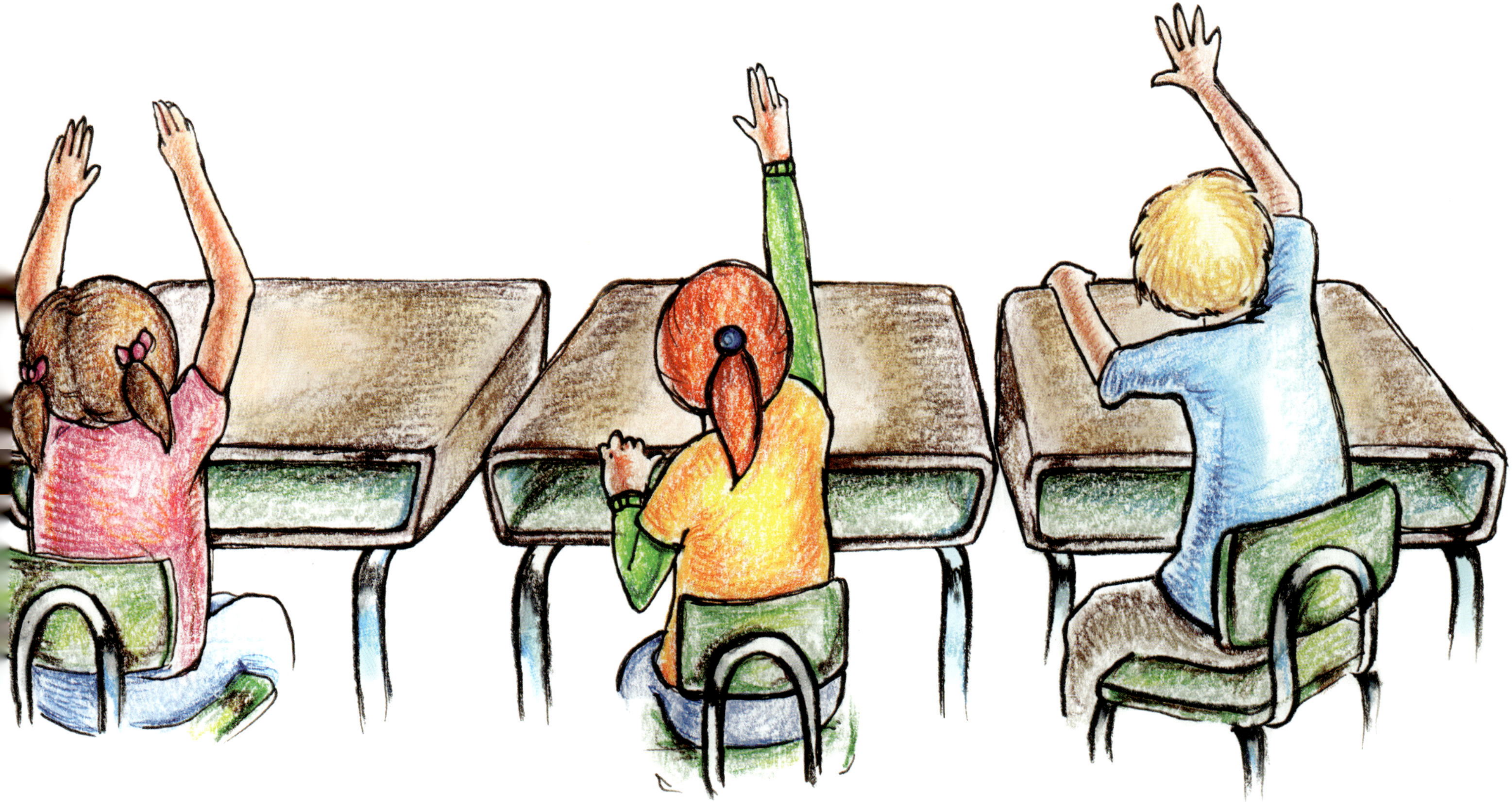

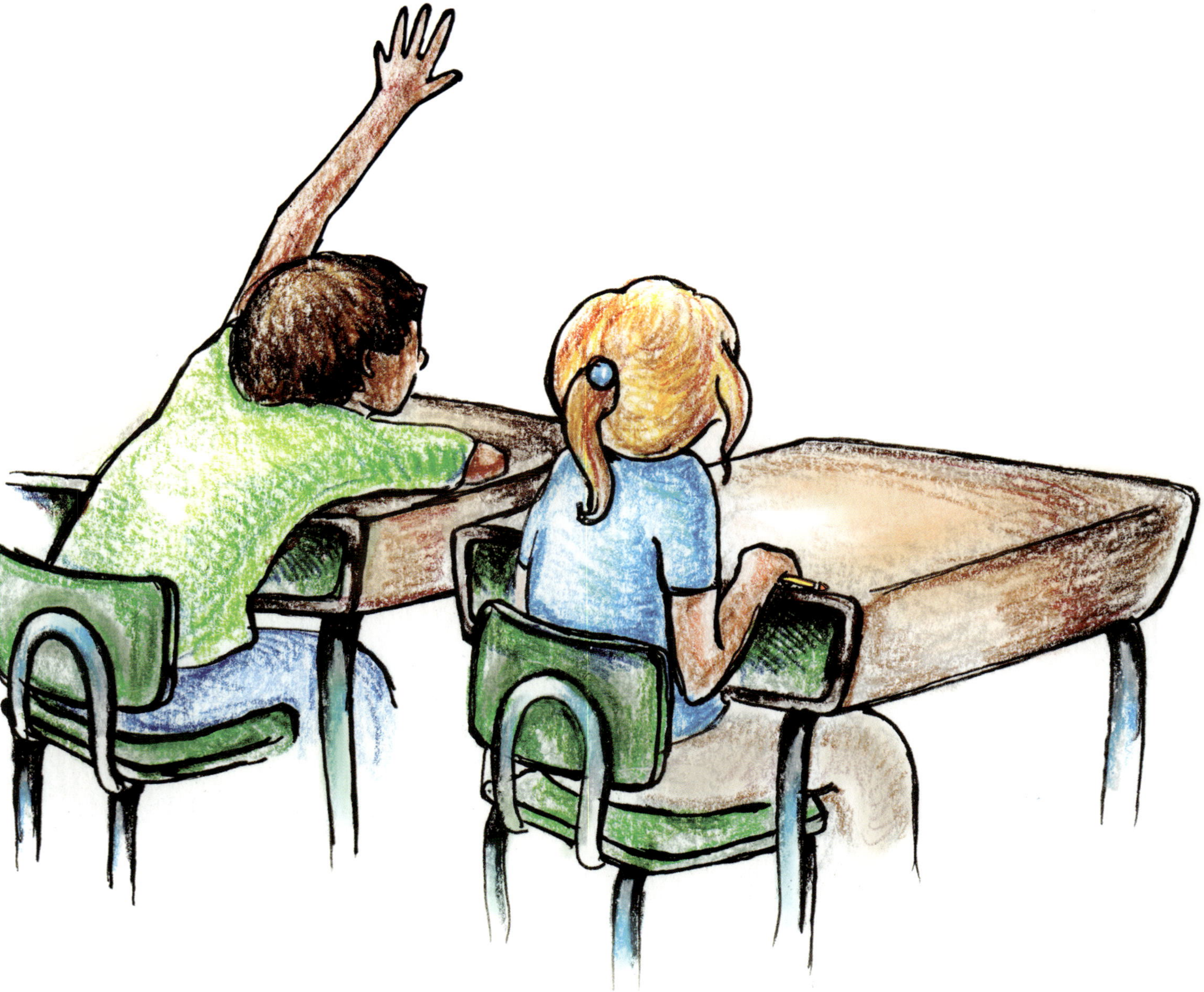

Finally, they got a call from Mr. Adams. Even though it took several days for the buses to get to the Gulf Coast, they did make it!

By the time the water got there, another hurricane named Rita had developed and caused even more damage to the same area. Their donations were able to help people involved in both storms!

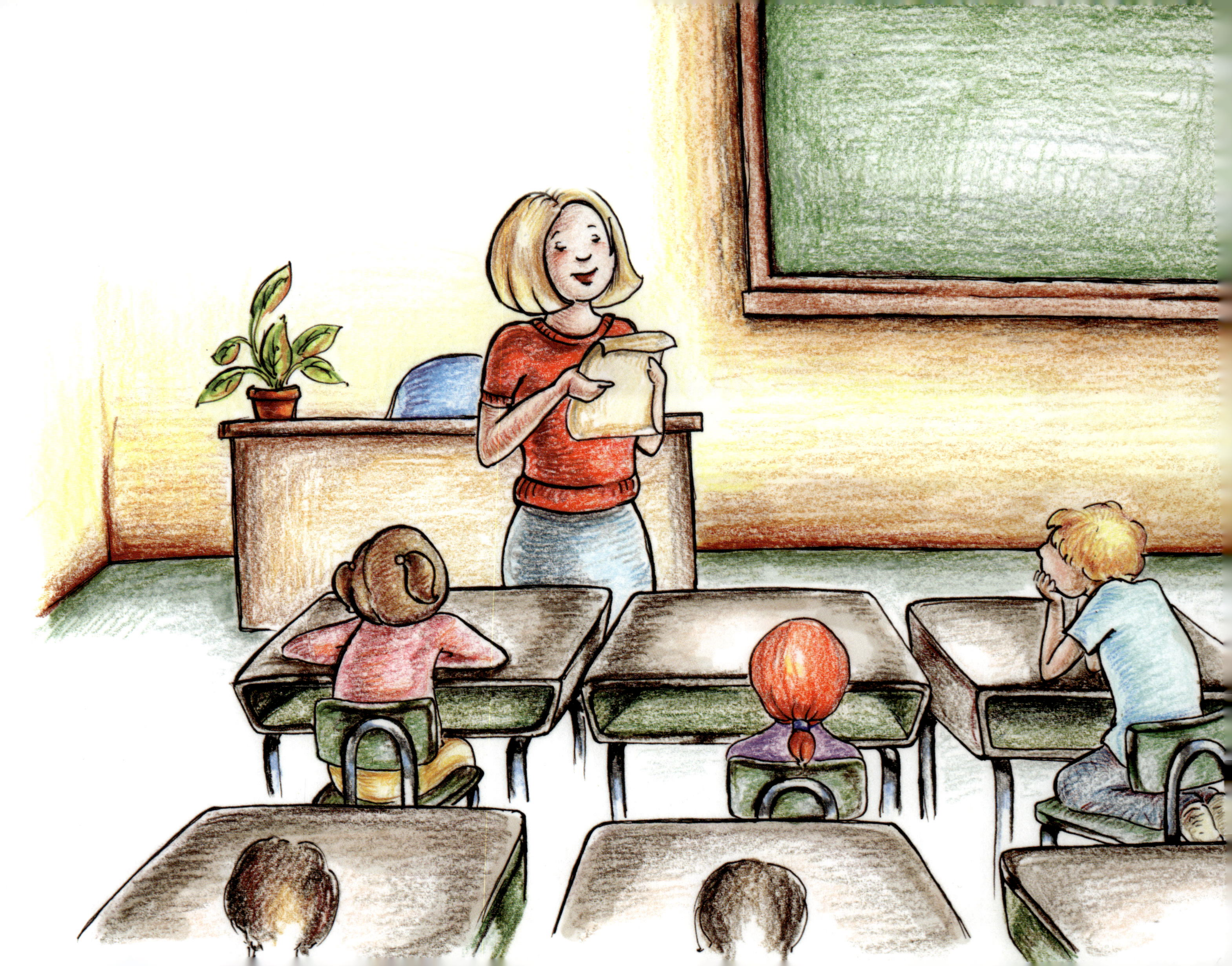

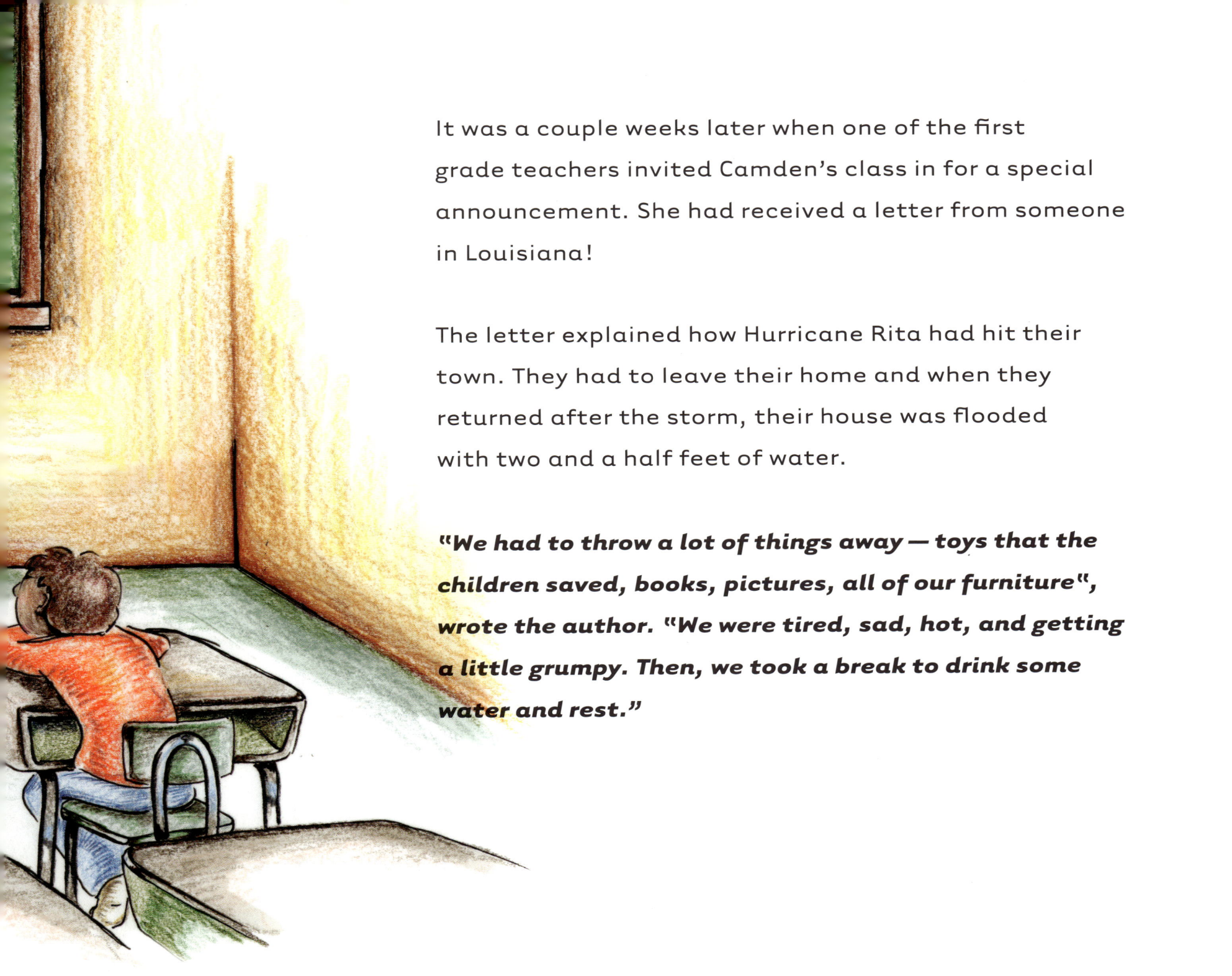

It was a couple weeks later when one of the first grade teachers invited Camden's class in for a special announcement. She had received a letter from someone in Louisiana!

The letter explained how Hurricane Rita had hit their town. They had to leave their home and when they returned after the storm, their house was flooded with two and a half feet of water.

"We had to throw a lot of things away — toys that the children saved, books, pictures, all of our furniture", wrote the author. "We were tired, sad, hot, and getting a little grumpy. Then, we took a break to drink some water and rest."

"When we got the bottles of water, they were from you. They had wonderful little notes. The notes made us laugh and cry. We didn't cry because we were sad; we cried because it was so nice of you to do this wonderful thing. We will always remember you and we will think of you and smile."

The school children listened carefully to the words in the letter. They were thinking about the fun they had had writing notes on the labels, and how neat it was when the bus drove up and they all cheered. They remembered how proud they were when the buses left the parking lot filled with their cases of water.

Mostly, they were thinking of this family they were able to help from eight hundred miles away. They turned the family's bad day into a good one. These children were the calm in the midst of a terrible storm.

up high. We were tired, sad, hot and getting a little grumpy. Then we took a break to drink some water and rest. When we got the bottles of water - they were from you - they had wonderful little notes - the notes made us laugh and cry - we didn't cry because we were sad - we cried because it was so nice of you to do this wonderful thing. We will always remember you and we will think of you and smile. We weren't tired anymore - we started working again. Any time that you can do something nice for someone - like helping a brother or sister with homework - opening a door for someone, carrying the groceries, just do it. These things make people smile and make their days better. And it makes you feel good to do something good.

Thank you very much, we will always remember you.

That night before falling asleep, Camden was reviewing the day in his mind.
"Imagine if we could get another chance to make a difference like that!"
The opportunity may come sooner than he thinks.

"WaterWorks" Project — September 16, 2005

Over 340 cases of water were collected and sent to Louisiana for the hurricane victims.

Those who made it happen:

Jesse Wharton Elementary School — Greensboro, North Carolina

Caldwell Academy — Greensboro, North Carolina

Greensboro Academy — Greensboro, North Carolina

Ed Adams Transport — High Point, North Carolina

Thomas Built Buses — Thomasville, North Carolina

Kent-Mitchell Bus Sales and Service, LLC — Hammond, Louisiana

Steps to Action — The "IMAGINE IF" Way

Identify Your Passion
If you find yourself thinking about a cause over and over again, you may have found your passion!

Make a Plan
Ask yourself questions about how to help your cause. Jot down your answers to these tough questions in a journal or notebook.

Activate your Plan!
Take your first step by telling a trusted friend, parent, teacher, or another adult about your plan. After your discussion, add some key points to your journal.

Give it Some Thought!
Generate more detail about your idea through research, brainstorming and identifying all aspects of your project. This is the time to make a good project GREAT!

Inspire others
Get more people involved once your plan is written. They will want to help you "take action" when they sense your excitement and see your well thought-out plan.

No obstacles!
When it comes time to carry out your project, follow your plan. If something goes wrong, think about ways to get past the obstacle and keep going! Stay true to your plan, and be flexible.

Extend Yourself
Extending yourself means moving beyond your comfort zone and opening up to new experiences. Allowing others to extend themselves by using their own strengths and abilities is true leadership!

Invite Others to Celebrate!
It is a great feeling to help someone else. Celebrate and say "thank you" to those who assisted in the effort.

Formulate Your Next Plan of Action!
Helping others is only one idea away from a reality and every time you accomplish a goal, you get better at setting and fulfilling the next. Keep your eyes and ears open for your next opportunity.